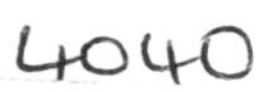

HISTORY OF
FAIRS AND MARKETS

RICHARD WOOD

WAYLAND

Books in the series

History of Canals

History of Fairs and Markets

History of Food and Cooking

History of Toys and Games

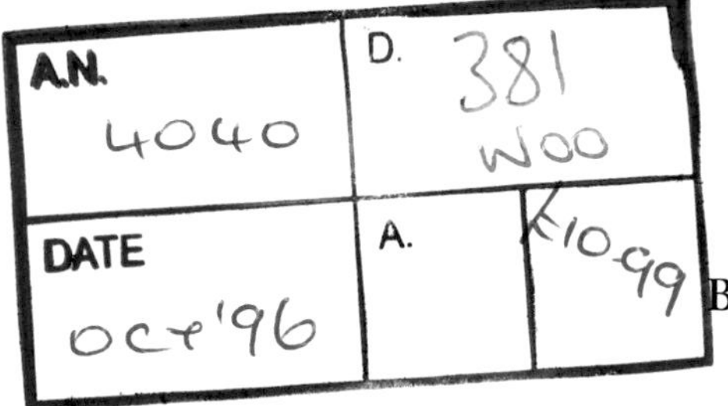

Series editor: Sarah Doughty
Book editors: Ruth Raudsepp/Louise Woods
Designer: Michael Leaman
Production controller: Carol Stevens

First published in 1996 by Wayland (Publishers) Limited
61 Western Road, Hove, East Sussex BN3 1JD, England.

British Library Cataloguing in Publication Data
Wood, Richard
History of fairs and markets
1. Fairs – Great Britain – History – Juvenile literature
2. Markets – Great Britain – History – Juvenile literature
I. Title
381. 1'8'0941

ISBN 0-7502-1680-8

Picture Acknowledgements
Bridgeman Art Library 5, 22, 24, 26, 27 (top); David Williams Picture Library 5;
E T Archive 14 (bottom), 18, 20, 21, 31; Eye Ubiquitous 6, 35, 43; © Gerry Yardy 29;
Hulton Deutsch 23, 25, 30, 34 (top and bottom), 36, 38, 39; Image Bank 33, 37; Impact 42;
Jorvik Viking Centre, York 13; Mary Evans Picture Library 17; Museum of London 9;
Norfolk Museums Service 14, 28; Popperfoto 41; Richard Wood 4, 15, 16;
©Rural History Centre 32, 36 (top), 40; St Albans Museums 10, 11; Tony Stone 7, 27 (bottom), 39 (top);
Universitetet I Oslo 12.

Typeset by Michael Leaman Design Partnership
Printed and bound in England
by B P C Paulton Books

Contents

Words that are printed in **bold** in the text are explained in the glossary on page 46.

Introduction

Market Day

You may be surprised that this book is about two such different things as fairs and markets. There is probably a regular market somewhere near where you live. You might shop there for fruit and vegetables, plants and flowers, fresh fish – or even for clothes, tools or household goods. Perhaps you just enjoy wandering between the colourful stalls, listening to the shouts of the market traders trying to persuade you to buy something. The market seems like a huge, bustling, noisy open-air shop.

▼ *This market stall scene, photographed in 1995, has changed little through the centuries. The half-covered stalls and the open display of produce would not have seemed strange in a Roman or Medieval market place.*

All the Fun of the Fair

Fairs today are still like markets in some ways. They take place in the open air, have many different stalls and the same sense of excitement. But what they sell is entertainment, with merry-go-rounds and dodgems, shooting ranges, coconut shies and side-shows. Unlike the market, the fair probably comes only once or twice a year. For a few nights the streets come alive, then the fair is packed up and taken to another stopping place along its route.

An Ancient Tradition

Fairs and markets are not new. Many have taken place in the same spot for hundreds or even thousands of years. Markets have always been regular events where people buy, sell and exchange food and local produce. Fairs were originally like huge markets. Just like modern fairs, they came once a year and lasted for a few days. People shopped at the fair for all the goods they could not normally buy locally. **Merchants** travelled great distances, sometimes even from abroad, to sell their products there. To help people enjoy the fair, entertainers – acrobats, fire-eaters and jugglers, 'fat ladies' and animal performers – came along too. Gradually, the entertaining side-shows began to take over the fairground and by the end of the nineteenth century, buying and selling had almost stopped. The modern funfair had begun.

▲ *The site of a market is often marked by a cross, such as this one in Culross in Scotland.*

◀ *Covent Garden Market in central London in the eighteenth century. This market sold fruit and vegetables.*

Feast and Fair

Our word 'fair' comes from the latin word 'feria'. This was a feast, or holiday when people had time off work to celebrate a saint's day or religous festival. This was an ideal time to hold a fair because most people were free to attend.

From Prehistoric to Norman Times

Prehistoric Markets

The first farmers of prehistoric Britain began to settle in small communities five thousand years ago. Most of the village people hunted, worked the land and made the things they needed, such as pots, tools, weapons and clothes. As villages grew bigger, some people specialized in making or doing particular things. Some spun wool, others made clothes and bedding from animal skins. Some trapped wild animals while others fished. To share and exchange what they produced, they set up markets. To begin with there was no money. People **bartered** with each other, knowing perhaps that a simple leather bag was worth the same as twelve small fish. By the first century BC, when Celtic tribes ruled Britain, money had come into use. Their small silver coins were modelled on the coins of Macedon in northern Greece, showing that trade had begun with more distant places, too.

▼ *Prehistoric people held fairs on top of Silbury Hill in Wiltshire. They carried goods to exchange along the ancient trackways which crossed the hill.*

Some of the things that prehistoric people needed were not found nearby. During the Stone Age, sharp edges for cutting up food and making clothes were scarce. Flint stones, found in parts of south and east England, could be shaped into sharp-edged knives and axes. Such items were valuable, and people travelled long distances to buy them. The discovery of metals, mainly in the west of Britain, created an even greater demand for trade with far-off places during the Bronze and Iron Ages.

▲ *Stonehenge was an important Stone Age religious site, built over 4,000 years ago. Fairs were held when large numbers of people met at places like this.*

The First Fairs

Regular fairs began at meeting places throughout Britain. Many of these were where ancient trackways crossed, often on hill tops such as St. Giles Hill, near Winchester or Tingley (which means 'assembly hill'), in Yorkshire. Others were held on boundaries between villages at spots marked with a special stone, such as Clachan fairs in Scotland ('Clach' means 'stone'). Prehistoric fairs were often connected with religion, for example at the burial place of a **pagan god** or hero. As well as buying and selling, games and entertainments took place to honour the dead person. In ancient Greece, the Olympic Games began as a fair in honour of the **Olympian**, Zeus.

The Romans Arrive

The Romans first came into contact with British people through trading. Celtic chiefs bought luxury goods such as wine and oil from the markets of Roman Gaul (France). British wool, metals such as tin and copper, and even slaves, were sold in Rome. But when Roman armies invaded Britain in AD 43, they opened up trade between Britain and the Roman Empire far more widely than ever before.

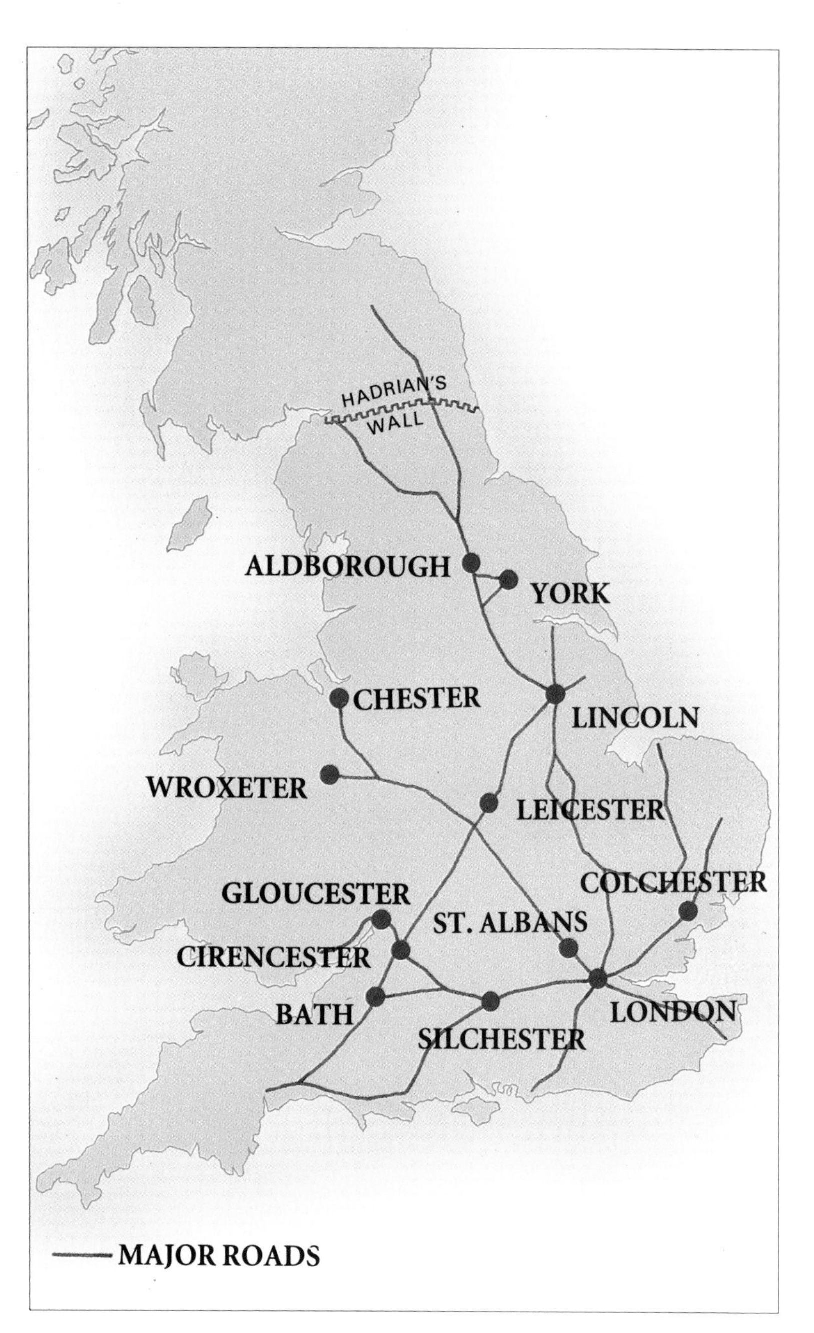

Trading Routes

The first fairs took place near ancient trackways. Prehistoric peoples used these 'green roads' for transporting their goods. But travel must have been painfully slow, particularly in winter when they were deeply rutted with mud. The Romans needed smooth, stone-surfaced roads to enable soldiers, messengers and supplies to get from one part of the country to another quickly. Though their main purpose was military, the new Roman roads gave a great boost to trade of all sorts. Regular markets were held in towns and villages along all the major routes, and in some areas fairs were set up to encourage trade with more distant places.

The annual fair on Newcastle Town Moor, which was started by the Romans, still continues to this day.

◀ *The main roads of Roman Britain. Goods from all over the Roman Empire were carried to market along these routes.*

▲ *A museum model of the riverside area of London in Roman times. Towns and markets often started at the point where deep rivers became narrow enough to be bridged.*

Roman Fairs

Merchants from across the Roman Empire came to Britain to buy such things as corn, animal skins, thick woollen coats called 'Birri Britannici', oysters, silver and lead. Rich Romans living in Britain demanded luxuries such as glassware from Germany, dried fruits from the Middle East, Samian ware pottery from Gaul, olive oil and 'liquamen' (strong fish sauce) from Spain. But Roman fairs were also connected with religion. They were sometimes held during pagan festivals such as Saturnalia, the midwinter celebration. We know that fairs in Rome often had side-shows with tents, booths and wooden platforms where people could watch entertainments. The fairground's mixture of work and pleasure had already begun.

Divine Protection

The pagan gods of ancient Rome all had special jobs to do. Mercury (also called Hermes) was the guardian spirit of fairs and markets. He was thought to protect travellers and watch over games. Mercury was also the patron of fortune tellers and pickpockets – also frequently found at fairs!

▲ *A reconstruction of the forum of Verulamium (St. Albans). People have gathered to buy from market stalls and watch entertainments.*

In the Forum

The Romans built many towns in Britain. At their centre stood a large open area called the **forum**. A network of straight streets spread out from here to the gateways in the town walls like the spokes of a wheel. The forum was the hub of town life and the main meeting place for its citizens. At one end stood the **basilica**, the headquarters of the town government and the forum was surrounded by covered walkways, shops and stalls.The open centre was the market place. Here, there were rows of makeshift market stalls, some covered, others open, where people could buy a great variety of produce. Much of it was brought in from the surrounding countryside during the early hours of the morning – farm carts were banned from the streets during the daytime. Other stalls belonged to craftsmen like potters, knife-makers and jewellers, who lived on the edge of the town and sold their goods from portable display stands. The forum must have been a bustling, noisy, and sometimes dangerous place. In some ways, a modern market shopper would find the scene quite familiar.

Market Laws

The Roman town officials could keep a close eye on the conduct of the market from the basilica. More recent markets, too, are often sited in front of a town hall or government building. From time to time officials checked the weights and measures used by the traders and punished cheats and thieves. Sometimes the government in Rome even tried to control the prices charged for certain goods, though this was hard to enforce. Market days and fairs in Roman towns were also the times when new laws and instructions were announced. Without any radio, television or newspapers, it was important to do this at a time when the greatest number of people would be present to hear what was said.

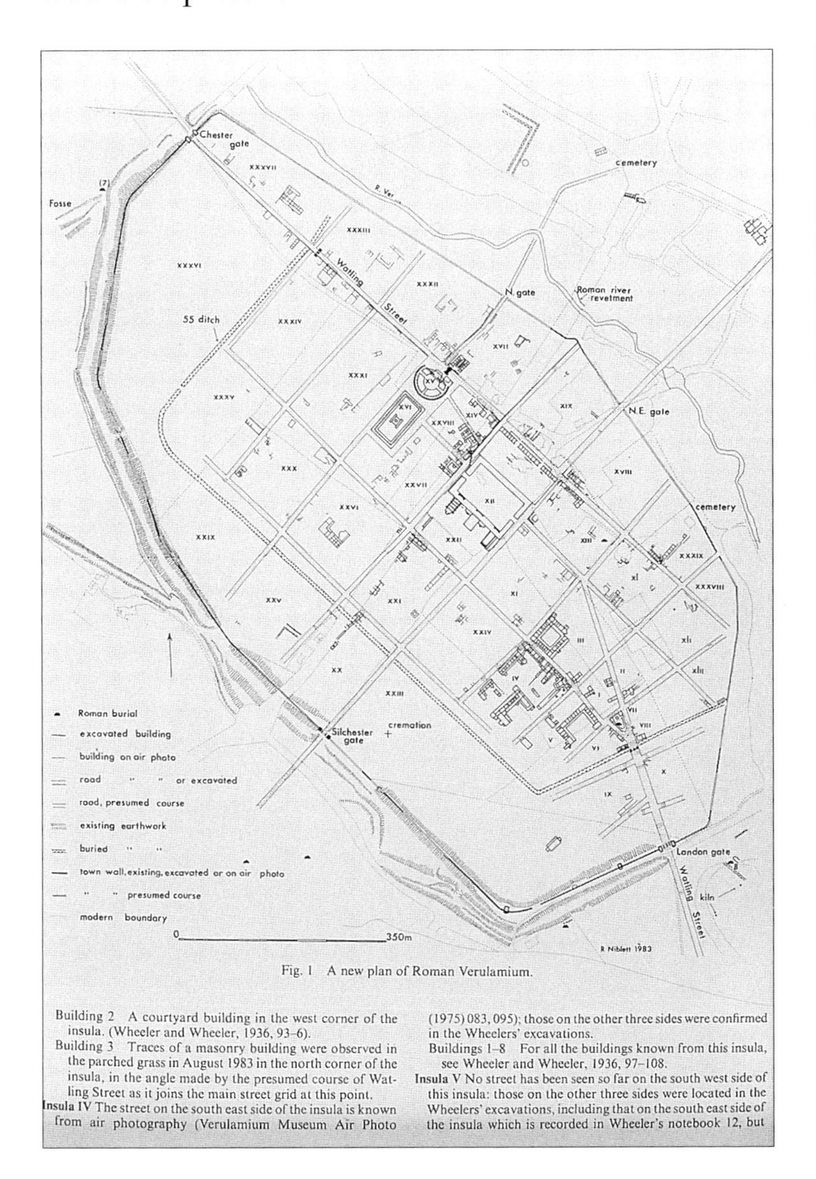

◀ *A plan of Roman Verulamium. Notice how the main roads into the town all met at the market place or forum in the centre.*

Bread and Circuses

From 71 BC, the poorest people in Rome were provided with free bread and entertainments. This was to try to keep them happy and prevent riots. The poor of Roman Britain had no such treats, and some went to market to beg for a living.

Roman Rule Ends

In AD 410, the Roman army was called away from Britain to defend Rome from attack. Roman officials and rich citizens soon followed. Before long, the fine buildings of the Roman towns lay neglected or abandoned. Much of the flourishing trade of the Roman fairs and markets disappeared almost overnight. The native Britons were soon joined by Saxon and Viking invaders. Mostly, these people lived in small villages which were largely **self-sufficient** in food and essentials. Though they had little need of the extensive trade of Roman times, markets still existed and some ancient fairs continued to meet.

▲ *Some of the goods which Viking traders sold in fairs and markets all over Europe.*

Sunday Trading

One Roman custom which survived was the Sunday fair. Sunday had been made a rest day by the Emperor Constantine. The practice continued, and with it that of holding fairs on this day. For the Christian Church, Sunday was a holy day. Buying and selling were frowned upon. The Saxon kings supported the Church and tried to stamp out Sunday trading – without much success. A thousand years later, this debate is still going on!

Means of Exchange

For a time, coins fell largely out of use and people returned to the barter system. Alternatively, small pieces of silver were used. These were weighed on a balance while an official watched to prevent cheating. For larger values, foreign coins were used, and by about the year 650 money was again minted in England. Tenth-century Saxon kings tried to control fairs and markets. King Athelstan (924–39) forbade the export of horses, Edgar (957–975) standardized weights and measures throughout England, and Edward the Confessor (1042–66) collected **tolls**. At Lewes fair, for example, both the buyer and the seller paid a half-penny to the king whenever an ox was sold.

Viking Trading Ships

The Vikings conquered northern Britain in the ninth and tenth centuries. With their sleek ships, they traded all over Europe and beyond. Their biggest market was at York, or Yorvik, which an English monk described as 'a city made rich by the wealth of merchants'. Today, the quayside market area has been reconstructed over the remains of the original settlement.

The Middle Ages

▲ *Pilgrim badges, such as this one, were popular souvenirs which people bought on visits to holy places. Some churches had the king's permission to hold fairs on important feast days when many pilgrims would be present.*

Market Charters

When William of Normandy conquered England in 1066, he looked for ways of controlling and profiting from his new kingdom. According to English law, all towns had to get the king's permission to hold markets or fairs. But in 1086, William found that only fifty towns had done so. He now insisted that a **charter** must be obtained before markets or fairs were held. This charter stated exactly where and when the market could take place. It laid down who could collect tolls, who could check weights, and who was to enforce law and order and punish criminals.

A Profitable Business

Charters were usually granted to churches or to powerful local people. In return for organizing the market or fair, they collected money from everyone who used it. As well as taxes on sales, there were charges for using stalls and fines from offenders. Fairs were especially profitable. They might last for several days and attract merchants from all over Europe. They were often timed to coincide with major religious celebrations, such as an important saint's feast day.

▲ *The Wife of Bath, a character from Geoffrey Chaucer's fourteenth-century 'Canterbury Tales'. Her bright dress and broad-brimmed hat were typical of the clothing sold at Medieval fairs.*

The Feast of St. Ethedreda

Ely fair lasted for six days at the feast of St. Ethedreda. Visitors bought cheap lace souvenirs. They were called 'tawdries' from Audrey, short for Etheldreda. Our word **tawdry** comes from this.

In 1110, King Henry I gave the abbots of Ramsey Abbey the right to hold a fair at St. Ives, near Huntingdon. The fair lasted for eight days every Easter, and before long it became the abbey's main money-earner. All the houses, stalls and booths were built by the abbey and rented out to traders. Twenty monks worked throughout the year to organize the fair. The abbots of Ramsey did all they could to encourage the fair. To persuade pilgrims to attend, they even found a 'holy well' with health-giving waters. By the 1200s, St. Ives Fair was one of the largest in the country. Even the king sent his tailors to buy cloth from the many foreign merchants who attended.

▲ *Norwich market is still held every day, next to the city's Medieval Guildhall. This building once held a courtroom and prison where market offenders were punished.*

The Peace of the Fair

With so many people gathered in one place, it was sometimes difficult to keep order. There was no police force, so the organizers of the fair had to enforce the law themselves. The abbots of Ramsey sent the **constables** from all their estates to St. Ives Fair and every large household had to appoint a watchman to guard the stalls. Visitors to the fairground were easy prey for pickpockets, known as 'cutpurses' because they cut off the purses that hung from people's belts. Drunkenness and fighting were also common at the fairground.

Other offences included dishonesty amongst the fair traders themselves. Some sold rotten fish, watered down ale, added chalk to flour or used false weights and measures. Travel to and from the fair could be dangerous too, especially for merchants laden with goods to sell. Charters often gave merchants a 'safe conduct', a sort of guarantee that they would be safe from attack on the roads.

Pie Powder Courts

To settle such matters, many fairs had a special court known as the Court of Pie Powder. This curious name came from the French 'pieds poudreaux'. This means 'dusty feet', and was a term used to describe the pedlars or travelling salesmen who visited fairs in great numbers. Permission to hold a Pie Powder court was usually given by the king and writen down in the fair charter.

The Pie Powder court usually met every day during the fair. The steward of the abbot or lord acted as the judge, but in towns the mayor usually presided. Common punishments were fines, public whipping or sitting in the **stocks.** Sometimes Pie Powder courts tried to make the punishment fit the crime. Brewers were made to drink some of their own bad beer. The rest was then poured over their heads! While this court was sitting, no other courts were allowed to take place, so the right to hold the court gave the fair holder considerable authority in the area. The last of these courts was held as late as 1898 at Hemel Hempstead.

Musicians and Acrobats

Wandering musicians, actors, acrobats and puppets often entertained visitors at Medieval fairs. Sometimes they used a cart for a makeshift open air stage, or performed in the courtyards of inns. As they could not charge for admission, they sent a hat round to collect money. Some people thought this was begging and tried to stop them. Others, such as the fifteenth-century Bishop of Salisbury, complained about their 'dances or vile games which tempt to **unseemliness**'.

▲ *Medieval trading ships. Transport of goods by land was slow and sometimes dangerous. The success of Medieval fairs such as Sturbridge depended on their easy access by boat to the sea.*

Sturbridge Fair

For centuries, the greatest English fair was Sturbridge. Though said to have been founded in Roman times, it was King John who granted its charter in 1211. From then until 1933, the fair was held annually near Cambridge. Sturbridge was well-sited, only fifty miles from London. The River Ouse brought traders from the north and from Europe. Merchants' carts arrived from the south and west along an ancient track called Icknield Way, where road and river joined. By the 1400s, Sturbridge Fair had overtaken all others.

The highlight of the fair was its proclamation, on St. Bartholomew's day (24 August). A procession came out from Cambridge led by the Town Crier, with the mayor, gentlemen and traders. Bands of trumpeters, drums and bells played all the way. When they reached the site, the charter was read out, the fair declared open and the officials sat down to feast on fresh herrings.

Ceremonies like this were an important feature of many fairs. Trading was forbidden until the fair was opened, signalled by ringing bells and erecting a tall pole with a glove on top. While the pole stood, the Court of Pie Powder was in charge. To keep order, Sturbridge Fair was patrolled by eight scarlet-coated watchmen who called 'Look about you, there!' as they went on their rounds. Officials included the Lord of the Taps whose job was to sample all the ale.

Medieval fairs often lasted several days – Sturbridge continued for three weeks. Certain days were set aside for particular types of sale. The first few days were mainly for merchants doing wholesale business, later came the gentry, then poorer people. The last day of the fair was perhaps the most popular. This was horse sale day, with sports and races for entertainment. Sturbridge was so important that traders from all over Europe brought luxury goods to sell. People could buy carpets from Turkey, fine silk and delicate glassware from Italy and wines from France, Spain and Greece. There were furs from the Baltic and precious stones brought from the East by way of the markets in Moscow.

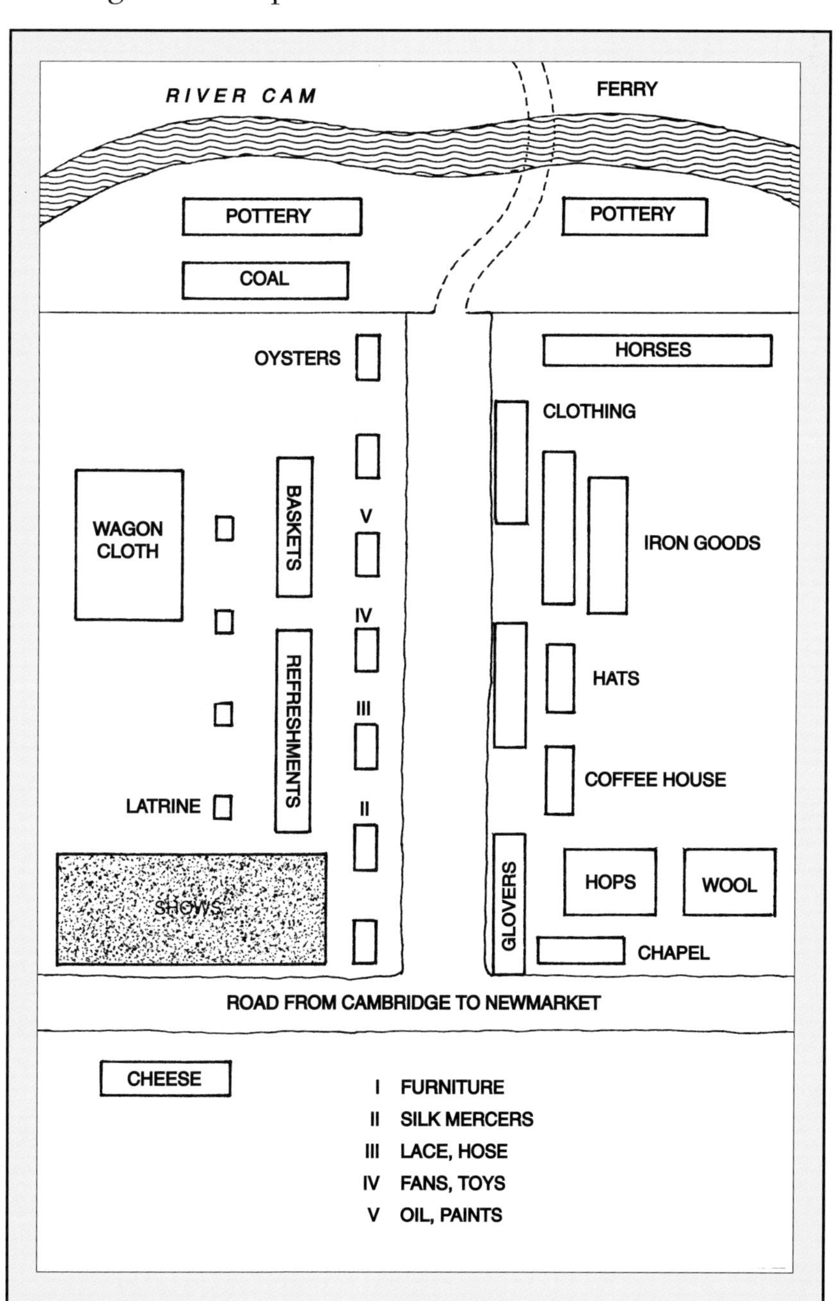

Sturbridge Fair

Sturbridge, like most fairgrounds, was carefully planned with a grid of 'streets' dividing the stalls. Separate areas were allocated to different goods and trades. Since few people could read, large signs were hung over the stalls. A boot stood for a cobbler, a knife for a cutler, a key for a locksmith. At the centre of the ground was a huge square called the **Duddery** where clothes and fabrics of all sorts were sold.

From Fairs to Markets

After about 1400, different parts of the country increasingly specialized in producing the goods they were best suited to. Some reared sheep while others grew cereals, some made cloth while others produced iron goods. This made communities less self-sufficient and more dependent on trade to supply their needs.

Regular local markets were the best way to supply people's needs. By the end of the Middle Ages the great fairs were declining in importance while markets were booming. Some market-places spread over a wide area and, like fairs, were divided into separate areas for different products. Medium-sized towns often had more that one market. King's Lynn still has two market-places, one for the Tuesday market, the other for Fridays. Large towns like Bristol and Leicester held markets on every weekday. Big cities like Edinburgh and London had daily markets which specialized in just one product. In Edinburgh, the names 'Fleshmarket', 'Fruitmarket' and 'Fishmarket' are still place names today. In London, Billingsgate was for fish, Smithfield for meat, and so on.

▲ *A fifteenth-century fruit and vegetable market. With many small stalls, it was difficult for the town officials to prevent cheating by traders.*

Not all markets were held in official market places. Some, like street markets today, were set up along the edges of busy roads in town centres.

Weights and Measures

As markets became busier, the job of ensuring fairness became more complex. Attempts had been made as early as the 900s to standardize some weights and measures. Differences continued to exist, and could be very confusing. Until 1569, for example, a hundredweight in Manchester was 120 pounds (54.4 kg), not 112 as elsewhere. Scotland had completely different standards and terms of measurement from England. So the mayor of each town took charge of a set of standard measures – a rod and yard (for length), bushels (for dry volume), and a balance with pounds (for weight). He was supposed to check the traders' measures against these, but local variations made the law hard to enforce. Most towns also had 'market lookers' such as ale-tasters, leather-searchers and 'aulnagers' who fixed the value of cloth.

▼ *The Medieval market cross at Malmesbury, Wiltshire. Covered octagonal buildings such as this were often built round earlier crosses. The Malmesbury cross stands just outside the walls of the old Medieval Abbey.*

Market Buildings

Two buildings often dominated the Medieval market-place. One was the **tollbooth,** where the standard weights were kept. The other was the market cross, an open-sided structure which gave some shelter for officials to collect money and customers to discuss business.

Secret Poultry

Sales outside official markets were discouraged. In 1345, a law in London prevented people 'selling poultry in lanes, houses and elsewhere in secret'.

From Tudor to Georgian Times

New Opportunities

Between 1500 and 1800, the population and the wealth of Britain steadily increased. Merchants and traders perhaps benefited most from the long periods of peace. They could now afford rich foods and comfortable homes, and looked to the fairs and markets to provide them. During the 1700s, towns grew as new industries started. Safer transport along new roads and canals helped speed goods to market. During the Agricultural Revolution (1760–1800), farmers were able to grow much more food, and most of this extra food was sold through the town markets. Tradesmen such as millers and corn merchants benefited from increased business. As the elegant **Georgian** buildings round many market-places show, towns were flourishing as never before.

▼ *This painting by Lucas van Valkenborch (1530–97) shows a sixteenth-century market scene. Some of the fruits, like grapes and lemons, have been imported from abroad. Produce from the surrounding countryside is sold by farmers' wives from their baskets.*

The Changing Face of Fairs

Fairs had always been short-lived events, ill-suited to providing for the day-to-day needs of townspeople and from the 1500s onwards, the fairground slowly changed into a place of entertainment rather than trade. In the Middle Ages, the Church had run many fairs very profitably, but under King Henry VIII (1509–47), the Church lost much of its power. Henry closed the monasteries and sold their fair rights to merchants and townsmen who were more interested in promoting local markets than fairs.

Bartholomew Fair

In 1133, a monk and jester called Rahere started the great Batholomew Cloth Fair in London. Rahere himself performed there as a juggler in order to raise money for the poor. By the 1600s, 'Old Bartlemy' was better known for entertainments than for cloth sales. Roundabouts and big wheels were first seen there. There were acrobats and rope-dancers, puppet shows, a conjurer called Hocus-Pocus and Richardson's Travelling Fairground Theatre. For a penny you could have your fortune told, see a bearded lady or even a 'mermaid'. Food was available from greasy-pork stalls, washed down with cheap ale and gin. At one time the rich, even royalty, visited the fair. But by the 1700s it was mainly patronized by the poor. Seventy-two officers were needed to keep order, and in 1855 the fair was closed for ever by the City authorities.

▲ *London's Bartholomew fair lasted for fourteen days every August. By the 1700s, sideshows and entertainment had taken over from trading as the fair's main purpose.*

▲ *St. James's Fair, Bristol. Country fairs like this combined business with pleasure. Notice the visitors on the hand-turned big wheel behind the tree.*

Mop Fairs

Until the early 1900s, many workers were hired to work for just one year at a time. Around Michaelmas (29 September), the farming year came to an end. Farm labourers and servant girls dressed up in their best clothes and went off to special fairs. They stood around until someone offered to employ them for the coming year. To show what type of work they wanted, they wore a badge of their trade. A shepherd tied wool round his hat, a **carter** carried a whip, a thatcher pinned straw on his coat and a housemaid held a broom or mop. Such fairs were called 'hiring' or 'mop' fairs. When agreement was reached, the employer gave his new worker a 'fastening penny' to seal their agreement. Not everyone was successful, and many people tramped round from fair to fair until they eventually found work. Those who did not like their new jobs might offer themselves for work a second time as 'runaway mops'.

Unusual Fairs

Country districts of Britain sometimes had strange fairs with their own local customs. The small village of Shropham in Norfolk held an annual horn fair. This was mainly for the sale of items like cups, spoons and shoehorns which were made from animals' horns. But there was also music and dancing and a procession through the village carrying a special set of horns made out of sheep and cow horns. Two unusual fairs took place near Aberdeen in Scotland. Sleepy Market opened at sunset and ended an hour after dawn the next day. Aikey Brae Fair took place for three days every summer on a remote moor, twenty miles north of the town. It is said to have started when a pedlar fell into a river. He spread out his goods to dry and was surprised when people came to buy them. He did so well that he returned the following year with other pedlars, and the fair has continued ever since.

Frost Fairs

During the 1600s, the River Thames often froze over in winter. When the ice was strong enough, people set up stalls to sell goods and food. The illustration shows the frost fair of 1684 which lasted five weeks. Notice all the different entertainments such as skittles and skating.

Buying and Selling

Country markets sold a wide range of goods. As at Sturbridge, different things were sold in different areas of the ground. Some parts specialized in selling horses or sheep and were equipped with rings and pens where the animals were displayed. Some sold wool and cloth, perhaps in a covered building. In other parts of the market-place, foods such as cheese, vegetables or meat were sold. Meat was especially important. In some market-places, the **shambles**, or butchers' stalls, eventually became permanent shops with solid walls and shutters to let down for displaying meat at the front. Country people took along a few live chickens, or some butter and cheese, or lace collars and embroidery.

▶ *A Dutch market scene in 1563. Poultry and dairy products were taken to market by country people and sold directly from the baskets they carried them in.*

Specialist Fairs

Some fairs grew up round the sale of one particular product. The Nottingham Goose Fair was held every October when geese were fully grown and ready for eating. At one time as many as 20,000 geese were sold, having walked many miles to the fair, eating the grass by the roadside as they went. Such fairs were important local events celebrated with music and processions. Lady Godiva's procession at Coventry Fair began in 1678.

◀ *Billingsgate Fish Market, London, in 1808. Fish was sold on this site for more than a thousand years.*

London Markets

Because of its size, London was the first city in Britain to have many regular markets devoted to just one product each. Fish was sold at Billingsgate a thousand years ago, Smithfield became a meat market in 1150 and Leadenhall a poultry market in 1309. When King Charles II took the Spanish Ambassador to see Leadenhall Market in the 1660s his guest remarked, 'There is more meat sold here than in all the kingdom of Spain!' The Great Fire of 1666 destroyed much of the market areas of London. When the city was rebuilt, each product was allocated a fixed site, where it remained until recent times.

Covent Garden, in the centre of London, became a fruit, vegetable and flower market in 1670. The fashionable people who lived round the square disliked the noise and dirt of the market. Actors moved there instead and made Covent Garden a popular place of entertainment. In 1974 the market moved south of the River Thames. Today the old market has many small shops and cafés and hosts an annual Punch and Judy festival.

Victorian Fairs and Markets

During Queen Victoria's reign (1837–1901), Britain's population grew from sixteen to thirty-seven million. By 1901, most people lived in cities and worked in factories. Steam trains made the transport of goods and people easy and fast. There was less need for general country fairs, which gradually changed into the funfairs we know today. Markets in towns with good railway connections prospered. Those in small towns or out-of-the-way places declined or closed. During Victoria's reign, the number of places with regular markets fell from 550 to 350.

Livestock Markets

Until Victorian times, most towns were quite small. Their food came mainly from the surrounding countryside, either in farmers' carts or on four legs. Sheep, cattle and pigs walked themselves to market. Living animals, called livestock, were sold in special areas of the market. Meat, or deadstock, was sold at butchers' stalls and shops. As towns grew bigger, it was no longer possible to sell all the animals on the same market day. Towns would become filthy and dangerous with so many animals in the streets. Some markets chose a different day of the week for each animal, others had 'fatstock' days (for meat) and 'leanstock' days (for rearing and breeding).

▼ *Checking the animals at a Victorian country fair. The artist, Alfred Munnings, based this scene on Lavenham Horse Fair in Suffolk.*

Under the Hammer

After 1845, goods were often sold at markets and fairs by auction. The auctioneer rang a bell to start the sale. People then 'bid' by calling out or signalling the price they would offer. When nobody offered more, the auctioneer banged his hammer to show that the sale was made.

Livestock Fairs

Fairs tended to cater for just one type of animal. In eastern England there were several annual sheep fairs. People from all over Europe and even from America and Australia bought horses at Horncastle Fair. The biggest cattle fair was St. Faith's Fair outside Norwich. Most of the animals which ended up in London's Smithfield Market changed hands here. Beginning in Scotland, they slowly trekked south to be fattened up in East Anglia. They were sold again at Barnet or St. Faith's, then they walked to London.

A Social Occasion

Many visitors to livestock fairs had no intention of buying, but went to enjoy the scene. There were usually side-shows, amusements, competitions and games. Drinks and hot foods were on sale, and children took a day off school. At small country fairs, families and friends who did not often see each other met to exchange gossip and share a meal. Bigger fairs were important social occasions for the farmers and landowners, who attended a grand dinner with speeches. Major fairs often took over the whole town centre and provided a welcome boost for local business.

▲ *The covered market at Kirkgate, Leeds. Many large towns encouraged traders and shoppers to visit by constructing new market buildings like this.*

There were disadvantages, too. There were constant complaints about the dirt and smell of town-centre markets. A writer to the '*Farmers Magazine*' in 1856 complained that there were so many animals at Barnet Fair that it was impossible to walk down the main street.

Even the pavements were obstructed by animals left tethered outside pubs while their owners drank inside. Animals could be hard to control, as when a bull broke loose in Banbury Market and crashed through the window of a sweet shop. From early morning until late at night, the surrounding streets and country roads were choked with farm animals, carts and coaches.

Trains and Trade

Barnet, being close to London, was one of the livestock fairs which grew during Victorian times. The building of a railway made transport of live animals much faster. Cattle arriving by train from Wales and the north were fat, fresh and not worn out by walking. Prices were higher and the fair flourished. Smaller fairs and those which did not have a big city or a railway line nearby, suffered. Many closed altogether. In 1792, there had been 130 fairs in Kent. By 1888, there were just thirteen left. The same was true of weekly livestock markets and many small ones closed. By 1901, most remaining livestock markets had moved out to special sites on the edge of towns.

New Types of Fair

Queen Victoria opening the Great Exhibition of 1851 in Hyde Park, London. New inventions and industrial goods were displayed at vast trade fairs like this.

People flocked to the Great Exhibition from all over Britain and from Europe to marvel at the displays of goods from around the world.

The Corn Trade

Millers and bakers were always in need of fresh corn and flour. This made corn more suitable for selling at weekly markets than at annual fairs. On fine days, business was conducted in the open. But in wet weather, cover was needed or the corn would be spoiled. Some towns still had old market cross buildings to shelter the dealers. Alternatively, the yards and upper rooms of inns round the market-place provided a comfortable place for business to be conducted.

Corn Halls

The spread of railways during the 1840s and 50s resulted in fewer but larger corn markets. Many towns encouraged trade by building special corn exchanges. These were big, covered market buildings with space for dealers to set up stands and display samples or sacks of corn. Towns often competed with each other to see who could erect the grandest hall. In ten years from 1847, fourteen new corn exchanges were built in Lincolnshire (a major corn-growing area). Grantham built two, both big enough to seat 800 people. Many Victorian corn halls still dominate our market places today – though not used for their original purpose.

▼ *Farmers selling sacks of corn from open carts in an early Victorian country market. With the coming of railways, the corn trade concentrated in larger towns with covered corn halls.*

◀ *A London street market today. In Victorian times, too, market stalls often spilled over into the streets round the market-place.*

The General Market

The town centre market was the one for ordinary shoppers. Until Victorian times, such markets sold almost everything people needed. But as more and more shops opened, the sale of clothes, pots and pans, books and factory-made goods became the business of shopkeepers rather than market traders. Though many markets specialized in cheap food, there were usually **hawkers** or **chapmen** (meaning market men) selling anything from pocket knives and crockery to padlocks and 'chapbooks' – children's stories with crude illustrations. Some chapmen travelled from market to market and were well-known for their 'cries' as they tried to persuade people to buy their goods.

Better Conditions

In the 1850s, the cramped and dirty conditions in some markets were improved as people became more aware of health risks. Some towns, like Lincoln and Liverpool, built covered markets to protect shoppers from the weather, and organized for rubbish to be collected at the end of the day. Others paved their market places which meant they could be easily swept, or washed down with water. Shopping in the market was far more pleasant and safer than a century before.

▲ *Nottingham Goose Fair in 1873. By Victorian times, geese were hard to find. Instead, plays, music, sideshows and foodstalls made this one of the largest funfairs in England.*

Victorian Funfairs

By 1900, buying and selling at general fairs was almost over. Thanks to better transport, shopkeepers did not need fairs to purchase stock. Country people who had once relied on fairs for household goods could now travel to town by train and shop whenever they wished. Only special fairs like mop and horse fairs survived in their original form. As the traders and shoppers abandoned the fairground, their pitches were taken over by entertainers. By 1901, the word 'fair' was, to most people, short for 'funfair'.

Fairground Entertainers

As pleasure fairs grew, the number and variety of entertainments increased. Strong ladies, conjurers, wrestlers and puppet shows travelled from fair to fair. Some shows gave people a chance to take part, perhaps by throwing a wet rag at an **aunt sally** or knocking coconuts off the shies. Until the 1840s, the only plays most people saw were twenty-minute 'penny gaff' performances in 'canvas theatres' at fairs. Edmund Keane, who became a great actor, began his career performing at Richardson's Travelling Fairground Theatre.

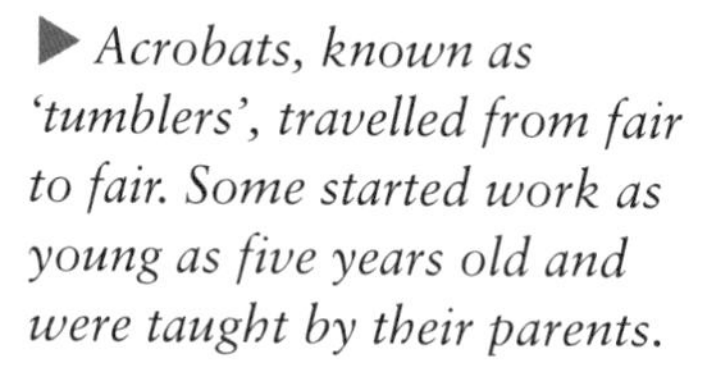

▶ *Acrobats, known as 'tumblers', travelled from fair to fair. Some started work as young as five years old and were taught by their parents.*

Complaints

Some parents dreaded the arrival of the fair in town. Victorian boys and girls were not supposed to meet unless their parents were present. The fair gave them an ideal opportunity to get together out of sight. The large crowds in town could be difficult to control. They also attracted criminals. A newspaper report about Abingdon Fair complained that 'pickpockets, highwaymen and swindlers made a much larger display than usual'. Public protest led to many small fairs closing during the 1870s.

▼ Colourful mechanical organs also toured the fairgrounds. They were originally hand pumped, but later steam powered.

Animal Shows

Performing wild animal shows, or menageries, travelled round many of the big Victorian fairs. The two largest were Wombwells and Atkins, which competed to provide the most unusual animals. Atkins' show included lions, tigers and leopards, two zebras, pelicans and porcupines and a laughing hyena. People paid one shilling (5p) to see them, or sixpence for 'working people'. Conditions were not good. Wombwells' elephant died while walking from Newcastle to London. Not one to lose money, Mr. Wombwell then displayed its body as a highlight of the show, a dead elephant being rarer than a live one!

▲ *A merry-go-round from the early 1800s. The riders are seated on wooden horses. Two ladies are peering out of a model carriage. You can just see the men pushing it between the horses.*

The Provincial Fair

For many people, the annual fair in the local market town was the highlight of the year. For a few days, the town came alive with unfamiliar sights, sounds and smells. Shops stayed open late, drinks and hot foods were available from special bars all day long. There was an air of excitement as the first showmen began to arrive in their brightly painted horse-drawn caravans. Their job was to set up the tober, as they called the fairground, dividing it into 'pitches' for different shows. The larger tents and open-air amusements were in the centre, with smaller booths as side-shows on the outside. The showmen's living quarters were parked on a separate ground nearby. The whole ground was then hung with flags and bunting, and lit with portable lanterns so that the fair could continue late into the night. Once the fair was declared open at a special ceremony, strangers from surrounding areas began to flood in. Mostly they walked, but from the 1840s many arrived by steam train on special cheap excursion tickets.

▶ *Powerful steam engines enabled merry-go-rounds to become much bigger by the end of the nineteenth century. Notice how the people going to St. Giles' Fair in Oxford have dressed up for the occasion!*

Fairground Rides

By Victorian times, many fairs had rides and merry-go-rounds. 'Twigden's Riding Machine', built in 1855, was a simple roundabout turned by a man standing in the centre. Alternatively, small boys ran round pushing it, with free rides as payment. Larger roundabouts might have a mechanical turning device, operated by a man with a handle. People rode on wooden galloping horses, known as **gallopers**. In 1865, a showman at Aylsham Fair in Norfolk had the idea of connecting up the handle to a steam engine. This made much larger roundabouts possible, and before long, no fair was complete without at least one set of 'steam gallopers'. Music was provided by a mechanical organ in the centre, also steam powered. Fairground organs are still a popular feature of many fairs today.

▲ *Fairground horses, called 'gallopers', were painted in bright colours.*

Gig Fairs

Larger fairs, like Nottingham Goose Fair, sometimes had a special **gig** fair. This was one afternoon when wealthy people visited the fair, arriving in gigs and carriages. Prices were higher, and poorer visitors stayed away until the gig fair was over.

The Twentieth Century

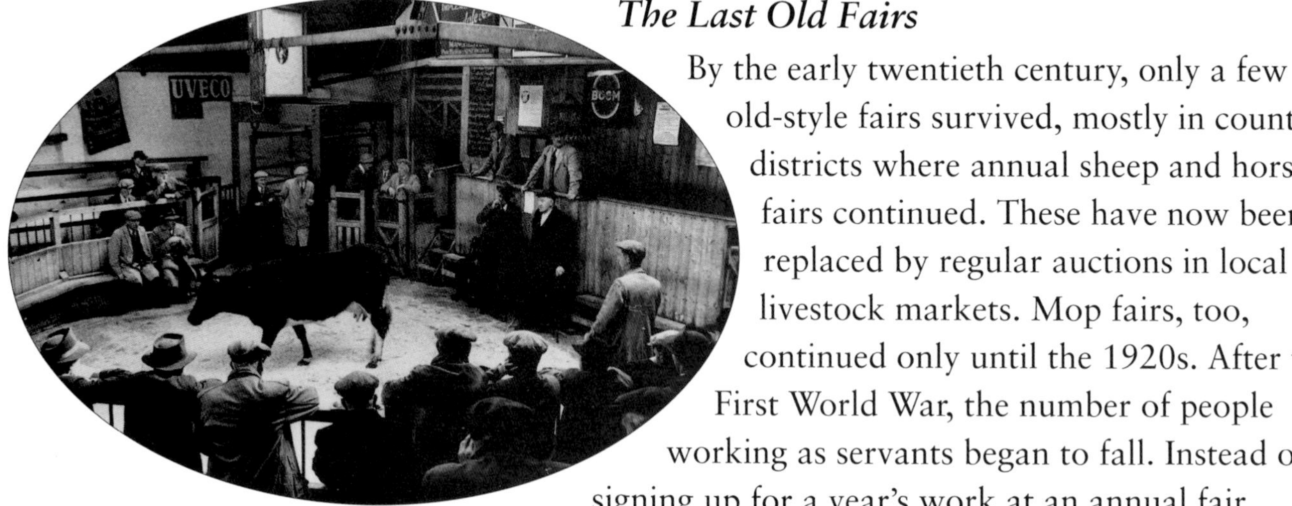

▲ *A Lancashire cattle auction in 1955. After the Second World War, most livestock sales moved away from public market places to covered auction rooms.*

The Last Old Fairs

By the early twentieth century, only a few old-style fairs survived, mostly in country districts where annual sheep and horse fairs continued. These have now been replaced by regular auctions in local livestock markets. Mop fairs, too, continued only until the 1920s. After the First World War, the number of people working as servants began to fall. Instead of signing up for a year's work at an annual fair, most people found work instead through newspaper advertisements or employment agencies.

Links with the Past

Despite their change of purpose, most fairs and markets have traditions which stretch back centuries. Fairs like Aikey Brae in Scotland and Newcastle Town moor still meet on the same spot where they began hundreds of years ago. Others still take place on the days laid down in their Medieval charters. St. Giles' Fair in Oxford, for example, lasts for two days on the Monday and Tuesday following the first Sunday after St. Giles' Day (1 September). Like many old fairs, it was originally set up to celebrate a religious festival. The festival may have been forgotten, but the fair continues.

▶ *Portabello Road street market in London is a popular place to hunt for unusual clothes and antiques.*

Street Markets Today

Street markets are still a common sight in Britain. Even fictional Albert Square in *EastEnders* has one! Until the Second World War, the Caledonian Market had over 2,500 stalls selling everything from kitchen tools to antiques. It still continues every Tuesday and Friday but on a new site in Tower Bridge Road. Nearby, Farringdon Street market specializes in old books and prints. Many London streets have Sunday markets. Petticoat Lane sells mainly clothing; Club Row sells pets; Sclater Street has a bird market. There are few things you cannot buy on the streets of London.

▲ *Covent Garden in about 1915. The bustling atmosphere of this fruit and vegetable market changed little throughout the centuries. Today it has moved to a new site, south of the river Thames.*

Ancient Customs

Some old fairground customs are still very much alive. The **Michaelmas** Fair at Egremont in Yorkshire is known as the 'Crab Fair'. The fair opens, as in the past, with crab apple throwing. The custom goes back to the Middle Ages when the Lord of the Manor used to ride round the fairground, throwing apples to the villagers.

Fairground Technology

Steam power and, by the early 1900s, electricity have done more than anything to change the look of the fairground. Without them, it is doubtful if fairs would have survived at all. Rides had once been small side-shows, no bigger than one man could push. With steam power, they became the most popular attractions of the fair. This was largely due to the invention, by an engineer called Frederick Savage, of the 'centre truck'. This is the central part of a roundabout which spins a hub called a 'cheese wheel'. Spokes stick out from the hub, from which the horse-shaped seats hang. Today, the traditional gallopers which Savage made have often been replaced with other shapes – cars, aeroplanes or spaceships.

▼ *The 'tober' of a town fair in the 1930s. Setting up the fair demanded co-operation and many hours of hard work by the fairground families.*

New Rides

Roundabouts can only turn horizontally. Big wheels, however, turn vertically and give riders a sense of flight. As early as the 1600s, there were small hand-operated examples at Bartholomew Fair. By the 1900s, with electric power and strong steel construction, gigantic wheels and roller-coaster rides had become possible. The biggest examples are set up at permanent sites such as Battersea Funfair, in London or at seaside towns such as Blackpool and Great Yarmouth. It would be impossible to move such monsters from place to place every few days. The dodgems are among the most popular rides at modern temporary fairs. These were invented in 1927 and have the advantage over most rides of being controlled by the rider.

Bioscope Shows

It was at King's Lynn Mart in 1895 that the British public first had a chance to see moving photographs or films. In the early years of the twentieth century, most fairs included a '**bioscope** show', as it was called. Fifty people would cram into a darkened tent to watch a few minutes of flicking black and white pictures, either silent, or with a mechanical organ for accompaniment. After 1907, when the first permanent cinema opened in London, films ceased to be a novelty. By the 1920s, they had gone from the fairground.

▲ *This picture shows the big wheel at the funfair which was permanently based in Blackpool in 1897.*

A Showman's Life

Working on a travelling fairground may seem exciting. But the life has always been a hard one for fairground workers, forever erecting, dismantling and repairing equipment. Most of this work is never seen by the public. Fairground families are constantly on the move, trekking from one site to another throughout the year. Whatever the weather, 'the show must go on'. Home for them is a travelling wagon. Wagons might seem cramped to a house-dweller, but most are comfortable and airy, with under-floor heating, well-equipped kitchens, and bathrooms. Fairground families usually know each other well and stick together, with children following their parents in the trade.

▲ *A showman photographed outside his home in 1994. Fairground families are constantly on the move, travelling from place to place in Britain, according to an annual fair timetable.*

The Showmen's Guild

In 1889, Parliament planned to restrict the use of caravans. This would have made the lives of fairground families almost impossible. A group of showmen formed an association, later called the Showmen's Guild, to defend their interests. They were successful in defeating the measure. Today, the Guild helps fairground families to keep in touch with each other. 'The World's Fair' is a weekly newspaper published by the Guild. Its features and adverts for new equipment, reports of fairs and details of events, make it the 'Showmen's Bible'.

▲ *The 'Looping Star' at Strathclyde Country Park in Scotland. Rides like this are not for the faint-hearted. Any fault could be dangerous and the law now requires regular safety checks.*

Fairground Safety

Machines which are regularly dismantled and checked are normally safe. This was not always true of fixed rides at permanent fairgrounds. In 1972, part of the big dipper at Battersea Funfair collapsed, killing several people. The Showman's Guild now insists on regular checks of all rides by trained engineers. Rides which do not pass the test are immediately stopped.

Perhaps nothing will ever stop the thrill which we, like our ancestors, feel when we go to the fair. For over two thousand years, fairs and markets have met at sites all over Britain. The goods and entertainments we find today may be very different from those of earlier times, but the old mixture of business and pleasure remains.

Timeline

3000 BC	2000 BC	1000 BC	100 BC	AD 43
First farmers settle in villages and barter their products.	Bronze tools sold by travelling smiths.	Iron goods traded at fairs on ancient trackways.	Celtic tribes use money and trade with Romans.	Romans settle in Britain. Foreign luxuries sold in British markets.

1066	1200	1330	1450
Normans conquer England. Only fifty towns have markets. King William I controls location of new markets.	Royal charters grant permission to the Church to hold fairs. Sunday trading discouraged.	King Edward III sets up wool markets.	Markets become more important than fairs for trading goods. 

1748	1780	1845	1850	1865
681 English towns hold regular markets.	Many people move to towns during the Industrial Revolution.	Auction sales start at many markets and livestock fairs.	Railways boost some markets but others close. Many towns build corn exchanges.	First steam-powered fairground ride.

100	410	900	1050
New Roman roads make trading easier. Markets centred in towns.	Romans leave Britain. Saxons arrive.	Vikings develop trade with Scandinavia. 	Market tolls collected for King Edward the Confessor.

1540	1563	1600	1666	1700
Most fairs now controlled by towns or lords.	Many mop fairs started by the Statute of Apprentices.	First round-about at Bartholomew Fair.	London markets move to new sites following the Great Fire.	Entertainments increasingly replace buying and selling at fairs.

1895	1900	1927	1930	1972
First fairground bioscope show. 	Only 350 towns have regular markets.	Dodgems invented.	Hiring of servants at mop fairs ended.	Fairground safety improved after accident at Battersea Funfair.

Glossary

Aunt sally
A fairground game where sticks or wet rags are thrown to smash a pipe in the mouth of a wooden figure.

Bartered
Exchanged one thing for another.

Basilica
A large building used by Roman town officials.

Bioscope
The Victorian word for cinema.

Carter
Someone who transported goods by horse and cart.

Chapmen
Men who travelled between markets buying and selling.

Charter
A document which gives rights to town officials to hold a market.

Constables
People who enforced laws and kept order at fairs.

Duddery
An area at a fair where clothes and fabrics were sold.

Forum
The square at the centre of a Roman town.

Gallopers
Wooden horses on fairground rides.

Georgian
The times of King George I to IV (1714–1830).

Gig
A two-wheeled horse-drawn carriage.

Hawkers
Market salesmen who shouted to sell their goods.

Merchants
Traders who buy and sell goods for profit.

Michaelmas
The feast of St. Michael held on 29 September every year.

Olympian
The description given to a Greek god. Mount Olympus in Greece is the home of the Greek gods.

Pagan god
A god or idol who is not recognized by the main religions of the world.

Self-sufficient
Communities able to supply enough food for themselves from their land.

Shambles
The part of a market place with butchers' stalls.

Stocks
A wooden frame with holes for the feet, head and hands into which thieves were locked as punishment.

Tawdry
Cheap and showy.

Tollbooth
The town hall or place where tolls were collected.

Tolls
Taxes paid on goods bought or sold.

Books to Read

Adams, S: *Trade and Religion, AD 453–1450* (Kingfisher, 1991)

Johnstone M: *Fairground Family* (A & C Black, 1985)

Lines, C: *Exploring Shopping* (Wayland, 1988)

Steel, B: *Medieval Markets* (Wayland, 1989)

Tanner, G: *Going to the Fair* (A & C Black, 1992)

Index